Little Mitchie

SAYING HELLO TO SOMEONE NEW

MAKING NEW FRIENDS

ANNE ACCARDI

CREATING YOUNG NONFICTION READERS

Little Mitchie books spark curiosity and support early nonfiction reading for students in Grades 2-3. Designed to build vocabulary, support second language learners, and prepare readers for middle-grade content, each book includes helpful tips for parents and educators to build confidence and deepen understanding of the world.

TIPS FOR READING NONFICTION WITH BEGINNING READERS

Talk about Nonfiction

Begin by explaining that nonfiction books give us information that is true. The book will be organized around a specific topic or idea, and we may learn new facts through reading.

Look at the Parts

Most nonfiction books have helpful features. Our *Little Mitchie* titles include color photographs and graphic aids, a table of contents, a glossary, and an index. Share the purpose of these features with your reader.

Color Photos and Graphic Aids

A lot of information can be found by "reading" photos, charts, maps, and other graphic aids found within nonfiction texts. Help your reader learn more about the different ways information can be displayed.

Table of Contents

Located at the front of the book, this list shows the big ideas within the text and the page numbers where they can be found.

Glossary

Located at the back of the book, the glossary defines key words and phrases that are related to the topic. These words and phrases can be found in the text in colored type.

Index

Located at the back of the book, an index is an alphabetical list of topics and the page numbers where they can be found.

With a little help and guidance about reading nonfiction, you can feel good about introducing a young reader to the world of *Little Mitchie* nonfiction books.

Little Mitchie is an imprint of:

Mitchell Lane PUBLISHERS

2001 SW 31st Avenue
Hallandale, FL 33009
mitchelllanepub.com

First Edition, 2027.

Author: Anne Accardi
Designer: Kathy Walsh
Editor: Kim Thompson

Library of Congress Cataloging-in-Publication Data
Title: Saying Hello to Someone New / by Anne Accardi

Description: Hallandale, FL :
Mitchell Lane Publishers, [2027]

Identifiers:
ISBN 979-8-89260-899-2 (library bound)
ISBN 979-8-90145-057-4 (paperback)
ISBN 979-8-90145-003-1 (eBook)

Library of Congress Control Number: 2026930166

Photo credits: Shutterstock: Cover, p 1 & 3, Roman Samborskyi; p 5, Denys Kurbatov; p 7, Nanci Santos Iglesias; p 9, Lithiumphoto; p 10, GagliardiPhotography; p 13, Milena Khosroshvilli; p 15, LightField Studios; p 16, BearFotos; p 19, Jacob Lund; p 21, Viktoriia Hnatiuk

TABLE OF CONTENTS

Step One

KNOW WHY GREETINGS ARE IMPORTANT . . . 4

Step Two

FACE YOUR FEARS . . . 8

Step Three

TAKE ACTION! . . . 12

Step Four

KEEP GOING . . . 18

TOP TIPS . . . 22

GLOSSARY . . . 23

FURTHER READING . . . 24

ON THE INTERNET . . . 24

INDEX . . . 24

Step One

KNOW WHY GREETINGS ARE IMPORTANT

Think about the last time you met someone new. What was the first thing they said to you?

They probably started with a **greeting**. Greeting someone is a great way to begin a **conversation**.

Greeting someone makes a good **first impression**. It shows that you are friendly, welcoming, and easy to talk to. It is the first step toward making a new friend!

"Friendship is the only cement that will ever hold the world together."
—Woodrow Wilson

Step Two

FACE YOUR FEARS

It can be scary to talk to a new person. Sometimes, taking the first step and saying hello is the hardest part.

It's okay to feel **nervous** or **shy**. The other person may feel that way too. Take a deep breath. Stay calm.

FRIENDLY FACT

When you greet someone, you let them know you are glad to see them.

There are many ways to say hello. If you are too nervous to talk, you can smile and wave. That is a way to be friendly without using words.

CHALLENGE

Find someone to wave to. What happened? Did they smile or wave back? How do you think a simple wave makes people feel?

Step Three

TAKE ACTION!

To greet someone, make **eye contact**. Say hello and introduce yourself. Give them a chance to share their name as well.

Next, share something about yourself. Tell them how old you are or what you're doing. If you can, mention something you both have in common. It could be a school activity or a hobby.

Try these ways to say hello.

- *Hey!*
- *Hi.*
- *Good morning.*
- *How are you?*
- *What's up?*
- *Nice to meet you.*

There are also **nonverbal** greetings, like a high five, a handshake, or a thumbs-up!

To keep talking, ask the person a question. This shows that you want to know them better. It shows that you want to be friends. You could ask what they like to do or how they feel about something.

CHALLENGE

Think of three questions you could ask people to get to know them better. Then, ask your questions to three different people. What did you learn?

FRIENDLY FACT

Smiling makes you happier! When people smile, they feel less stressed.

As you talk, make sure your **body language** is welcoming. Do not slouch, cross your arms, or look down.

Remember to smile. Make sure the **tone** of your voice is friendly.

Step Four

KEEP GOING

Now that you know how to say hello, you can greet many new people! They may be classmates, teammates, neighbors, or teachers.

FRIENDLY FACT

"What's up?" might be a great way to greet someone your own age. "Nice to meet you" may be better for a grown-up.

Go ahead and say hello to someone you don't know well. Soon, you will have a new friend!

TOP TIPS

Make eye contact.

Use a greeting.

Wave or give a high five.

Start a conversation.

Ask questions.

Smile!

GLOSSARY

body language (BAH-dee LANG-gwij) the thoughts and feelings your face and body communicate without using words

conversation (kahn-vur-SAY-shuhn) a talk between two or more people

eye contact (eye KAHN-takt) looking at someone when speaking to them

first impression (furst im-PRESH-uhn) the ideas and feelings a person has about you when they first meet you

greeting (GREE-ting) something friendly you say or do when you meet someone

nervous (NUR-vuhs) worried, scared, or anxious

nonverbal (nahn-VUR-buhl) without speaking

shy (shye) uncomfortable around people you don't know well

tone (tohn) the feelings and attitudes shown by the way you talk

FURTHER READING

Daniels, Natasha. *Social Skills Activities for Kids: 50 Fun Exercises for Making Friends, Talking and Listening, and Understanding Social Rules.* Callisto Kids, 2019.

Gregory, Kelly. *Say Hello.* Blue Balloon Books, 2023.

ON THE INTERNET

National Geographic Kids: How to Be an Awesome Friend
kids.nationalgeographic.com/pages/article/friend
Learn tips for making and keeping friends.

PBS Kids: Daniel Tiger's Neighborhood: Ways to Say Hello
pbskids.org/videos/watch/ways-to-say-hello/1764533
Watch a video to learn different ways to greet new friends.

INDEX

body language 17
eye contact 12, 22
greetings 4, 6, 12, 13, 19, 22
handshakes 13
introductions 12
questions 14, 15, 22
shyness 8
smiling 10, 11, 16, 17, 22